© **2018 Shawn Beaton All Rights Reserved**

ISBN: 9781728759012

Scripture taken from the New King James Version®. Copyright © 1982 by Thomas Nelson. Used by permission. All rights reserved.

Cover Images from Shutterstock.com

By Ollyy

Royalty-free stock photo ID: 317393642

Jesus

By Zbitnev

Royalty-free stock photo ID: 569969824

A crack in the monolith. Israel-United States relations

TABLE OF CONTENTS

It is unfortunate that we live in such a chaotic time. Words are flying out of the mouths of politicians with no thought or care for the damage they will create in society. For example, one politician said the followers of Donald Trump represent a small percentage of the American population and that they are a "virulent people" and the "dregs of society". How is this rhetoric any different than the words of Hitler? The person who spoke those words was the former Vice President of the United States Joseph Biden [i]. It is pretty terrifying when this language is given a pass, but it seems to have been given one. Where is the universal outcry against Joseph Biden and his hate filled rhetoric? In another surprising statement Hillary Clinton stated, "You cannot be civil with a political party that wants to destroy what you stand for, what you care about.[ii]" In other words Hillary Clinton is calling for revolution. But of course, she won't openly state that, but let her supporters and any radical groups interpret it as a signal to start attacking Republicans and to overthrow the elected government of President Donald Trump a Republican. You may have noticed that I cited two prominent Democrats. This is not accidental due to the fact that the Democrat party of old no longer exists, but it has become a godless party[iii]. When a nation or group of people forget God, they will become godless and will hate God's laws and those who teach them. The reason Joseph Biden and Hillary Clinton hate the Republican party and their values is based on the fact they reject the law of God. One cannot claim to love God or His law when he/she reject what He has written. The problem with the United States of America and other nations today is a division. A division becomes evident when the people hold two or more opposing visions. In the case of the U.S. it is basically about two visions as to whether they retain God and His laws in the life of the people and their elected government or rejecting His laws in the life of the people and their elected government. Those who reject God's laws are generally of Democrat party. The Democrat party has been hijacked by Socialists and Communists. These systems of government typically remove God from the national consciousness and their laws. What is taking place is essentially sedition and it began with Barack Hussein Obama. Like Lucifer who rebelled against God this man rebelled against the founding fathers and the U.S. Constitution they developed[iv]. President Obama was not an American president, but an imposter! He made it clear he was an imposter when he campaigned before his election in 2008, but most people don't follow words anymore. He wasn't running to enforce the laws of the land, but to change them. He stated in the 2008 campaign, "We are five days away from fundamentally transforming the United States of America[v]." He kept his promise by not enforcing the Defense of Marriage Act[vi] and only enforcing select parts of it. This is illegal because the law must be changed, but President Obama was lawless and chose what he would or would not obey. Under President Obama gay marriage became legal through the U.S. Supreme Court. The White House commemorated the day it was legalized by having lights displayed on it composed in the colors of the rainbow. This was a blatant rebellion against God's law and put America in opposition to God.

You shall not lie with a male as with a woman. It is an abomination.

Leviticus 18:22 NKJV

It is ironic that the president who signed into law DOMA was a Democrat! Bill Clinton signed onto this law, but he wasn't alone. Both the House and the Senate voted for DOMA with veto proof majorities! Clearly the Democrat and Republican parties were in favor of marriage as defined by God when DOMA was signed into law. But when President Obama came along he decided he didn't have to enforce this law and rebelled. The U.S. Supreme Court took this as a strong suggestion to change the law and deem it unconstitutional. The U.S. Supreme Court usurped DOMA and created a new law in line with Obama's desires. Obama refused to enforce section 3 of the law and the U.S. Supreme Court agreed it was unconstitutional. It should have been passed back to the legislature to be revised or changed, but the U.S. Supreme Court decided its job now included creating laws. The will of the people and God were overturned by the elite.

The Democrat party has become increasingly hostile to God's law while Republicans have been generally favorable towards it. The Republican party's support of God's law is no doubt a result of trying to please its Christian constituency. But many of the politicians in the Republican party are Christian and reflect the electorate that put them in power. The Democrat party has an electorate mostly composed of city folk while the Republican party reflects a more rural electorate. There is a clear division between rural and urban America. Rural America wants a more traditional America while the cities of America want a more progressive America. Many would argue that progressivism is basically another name for socialism. This is basically the practice of the Democrat party for it essentially sees its main purpose as overcoming every form of oppression. In addition, they generally desire to tax the rich and redistribute it to the poorer groups of the population. I believe the Democratic party once had noble causes to fight for, but most social injustices have been solved. The Democrat party has lost its ability to govern and has become a political group existing mainly for the purpose of protesting. They have nothing new to offer, so they stir up the people to be angry and to fear real or often imaginary forms of oppression. Apparently, the last form of oppression that must be removed is the patriarchy and the power behind it. The power behind the patriarchy is God the Father and the Bible. Both are antithetical to the many values of the Democrat party. Democrats champion feminism, abortion, homosexuality, transgenderism, socialism (not necessarily complete socialism) and a host of other issues. Many of these issues are incompatible with the Bible and God the Father also. The Democrat party knows it cannot be truly free to pursue their godless agenda until they remove God and Christianity from the U.S. Under Obama this seemed to be working, but their work was reversed when Donald Trump was elected president.

The election of Donald Trump was a rude awakening for half the nation who belonged to the Democrat party. They learned there was still a part of the population who didn't subscribe to their progressive views. One of the major reasons Donald Trump was elected was Barack Obama. Barack Obama left the U.S. with an economy that was barely moving along and a people who were more divided. Barack Obama alienated the Christian population in many ways and they finally woke up and ran to the polls on election day. In addition, the standing of America looked much weaker among the nations. There are few things Barack Obama achieved as president unless you consider the legalization of an abomination like homosexuality an achievement. That may seem harsh, but homosexuality really is an abomination. It is an unnatural act and a perversion.

When Donald Trump was elected the Democrats and some Republicans became hysterical and rightfully so. For Donald Trump would tear to pieces international agreements that compromised America's sovereignty and prosperity. Some of these agreements had been in place for decades. He disposed of NAFTA and bullied Mexico and Canada into a new agreement which was fairer to America. He took the U.S. out of the Trans-Pacific Partnership. He cut funding to the U.N. and the Palestinians. Moved the U.S. Embassy to Jerusalem ignoring Jerusalem's status as an international city under the jurisdiction of the U.N. Trump recognized Jerusalem as the eternal capital of Israel and of the Jewish people. President Donald Trump has also put in place two new U.S. Supreme Court justices and shifted the court to the right. Neil Gorsuch and Brett Kavanaugh are their names, and both are quite conservative. This seems to be the last straw for the Democrat party and now they are almost calling for outright revolution. Their attempts to link Donald Trump's election to Russian interference has failed. Their use of mobs and slander during Brett Kavanaugh's confirmation process failed to produce results. These attempts to halt Trump's return to Nationalism and its Christian roots have all failed. As a result, the Democrat party is looking for inspiration from a new breed of Socialists arising in the party.

In the 2016 election year the true winner among the Democrats was not Hillary Clinton, but the socialist Bernie Sanders. Hillary Clinton had no enthusiasm in her ranks, but Bernie Sanders did. It seems the old Democrat party died and a new one arose with socialism at its heart. Unfortunately, the new appearance of the Democratic party looks hip outwardly, but inwardly is a monster at heart. It is becoming a party that is opposed to capitalism and following the dangerous path of socialism. It is amazing that socialism is becoming so popular when the Trump economy has been so powerful and producing record results![vii]

I recently travelled to the United States and visited a friend. It had been some time since I last travelled by air, but everything seemed different. I felt as if I were all alone but surrounded at the same time. Very few if any interacted with each other at the airports I passed through. Everyone was busy looking at their cellphones and texting with an unseen person somewhere in the U.S. or the world. The real people around these texters were also unseen. Technology was supposed to bring us closer together, but in reality, it has made us more mechanical in nature. We are forgetting how to engage in face to face conversation and looking at a phone screen instead! I believe we have become enamored with these electronic trinkets and forgotten about the world around us. Many are aware of the trends and trendsetters in society but know little about history or political systems like Socialism. Our focus is misdirected toward the material world and as a result we are also misdirected towards systems like Socialism. Many have bought into the promises of free money and a redistribution of wealth without knowing the true costs of Socialism. The true costs of Socialism are the loss of freedom and prosperity. Freedom is lost because the socialist system is constantly overseeing everything to ensure all is fair. In such a system success or ambition is discouraged so that others do not feel inferior or disadvantaged. Financial success is punished with exorbitant taxes to reward those who have failed economically to ensure all is fair. Socialism proposes the illusory idea that it can make life fair for all but that is not possible. Every person has unique gifts and abilities. Some are more intelligent and others more artistic. Likewise, men have certain strengths as well as women.

How did the United States of America become so divided? The answer lies in the very same mistake President Donald Trump is about to make like others before him. He is proposing to make Israel into two nations. One that is Jewish or Israel and the other which is Palestinian or Palestine. The United States of America is under a curse of division because successive administrations have tried to broker a two-state solution in the Middle East by dividing Israel into two nations.

"For behold, in those days and at that time, when I bring back the captives of Judah and Jerusalem, I will also gather all nations, and bring them down to the Valley of Jehoshaphat; and I will enter into judgement with them there on account of My people, My heritage Israel, whom they have scattered among the nations; they have also divided up My land. Joel 3:1-2 NKJV

Any nation that decides to divide Israel will find itself at war with God Himself. Notice God calls the land His, but He has also leased it to Israel. In this passage of Joel, we discover that God judges every nation that scatters His people Israel or divides His land. How can we be certain that America is under a curse of division? Our answer lies in the Scriptures.

Now the Lord had said to Abram: "Get out of your country, from your family and from your father's house, to a land that I will show you. I will make you a great nation; I will bless you and make your name great; and you shall be a blessing. I will bless those who bless you, and I will curse him who curses you; and in you all the families of the earth shall be blessed." Genesis 12:1-3 NKJV

The basic interpretation of this passage is that God will do unto others as they do unto His people Israel or the land He has given them. Since various U.S. presidents have opted to meddle in Israel and tried to divide it in the name of peace God has also divided America. To divide Israel would make it smaller and not greater. God has called Israel to be a great nation. When America seeks to divides Israel, it compromises its own greatness. How can President Trump continue to make America great again by making Israel small? The spectacular economic period of Trump's first two years has been stellar, but only because he wisely chose to recognize Jerusalem as the undivided capital of Israel. In addition, it was due to his favorable treatment of the Church of Jesus Christ. But all these economic gains will be wiped out if President Donald Trump persists in fast tracking his plan to divide Israel.

At this time America is very divided and many of the leaders of the Democrat party sound as if they want blood! Their followers are listening and interpreting their words as a license to carry out violence against the Republican party. If Donald Trump pushes ahead with his two-state solution I believe it may seal America's doom. Either revolution, invasion, natural disasters or economic collapse will take place. In fact, all may take place and form a perfect storm that destroys America. The debt of America is enormous and unpaid. The stock market bubble is humongous! It wouldn't take much for this bubble to burst or for America's enemies to sell U.S. treasuries so that it defaults on its debt payments or its ability to fund its massive government. America looks strong on the outside, but any discerning eye can see it is teetering and ready to fall!

Like Babylon America is proud. It was pride that brought about Babylon's fall and this same sin is likely to bring about America's fall. Already the signs of America's fall as a superpower are everywhere. If it doesn't repent its fall will be complete and it will never rise to the greatness it once possessed. I will give you the reader verifiable signs that confirm that America is beginning to fail and fall as a nation and empire, but first let us look at ancient Babylon.

It shall come to pass in the day the Lord gives you rest from your sorrow, and from your fear and the hard bondage in which you were made to serve, that you will take up this proverb against the king of Babylon, and say: "How the oppressor has ceased, the golden city ceased! The Lord has broken the staff of the wicked, the scepter of rulers; he who struck the people in wrath

with a continual stroke, he who ruled the nations in anger, is persecuted and no one hinders. The whole earth is at rest and quiet; they break forth into singing. Indeed the cypress trees rejoice over you, and the cedars of Lebanon, saying, 'since you were cut down, no woodsman has come up against us.' "Hell from beneath is excited about you, to meet you at your coming; it stirs up the dead for you, all the chief ones of the earth; it has raised from their thrones all the kings of the nations. They all shall speak and say to you: 'Have you also become as weak as we? Have you become like us? Your pomp is brought down to Sheol, and the sound of your stringed instruments; the maggot is spread under you, and worms cover you.' "How you are fallen from heaven, O Lucifer, son of the morning! How you are cut down to the ground, you who weakened the nations! For you have said in your heart: 'I will ascend into heaven, I will exalt my throne above the stars of God; I will also sit on the mount of the congregation on the farthest sides of the north; I will ascend above the heights of the clouds, I will be like the Most High.' Yet you shall be brought down to Sheol, to the lowest depths of the Pit.**

Isaiah 14:3-15 NKJV

I posted these verses from Isaiah 14 to show the instigator of Babylon's pride. In this passage we see a king of Babylon is mentioned, but at the latter part of this passage a different being seems to appear. In fact, this being is given the name Lucifer and appears to be a spiritual entity. Most would agree with this assumption as the majority of Americans would associate the name Lucifer with Satan or the Devil. Lucifer appears to be self-willed and very proud. His pride is so great that he wants to exceed or become like God.

There are two sources of inspiration for life. One source of inspiration is God and another source is Lucifer. We are always faced with difficult decisions, but we can usually come to a safe conclusion as to what to decide based on the urges that are driving us. When God is urging us, it is usually to compel us to obey His written word known as the Bible. The Bible can usually guide us in most critical decisions. On the other hand, inspiration from Lucifer or Satan will urge us to follow our own way and not God's word. This is known as self-will or rebellion. The root of this kind of thinking is pride. Pride is the idea we know better than God or don't need His help or advice.

President Donald Trump and America are at a crossroads as a nation. When it comes to Mideast Peace will they go for a two-state solution and reject God's clear counsel or opt for an alternative course of action and seek His wisdom? The choice President Trump and America make will determine whether they continue to be great or be destroyed as Babylon of old was. In the

Proverbs we are reminded, *"Pride goes before destruction, and a haughty spirit before a fall"*, (Proverbs 16:18 NKJV).

One of the greatest strengths of Babylon was their great walls. These walls seemed to be impregnable, but when God determines the end of empire no wall or army can withstand Him. Ancient Babylon was conquered when an army entered the shallow waters of a river going through the city and moved underneath the walls. King Cyrus was victorious and seized Babylon with ease taking them by surprise[viii]. Even though Babylon's walls were high and thick, and they had several years of provisions it was not enough. Babylon would be conquered speedily, and its greatness was humbled. Babylon should remind us that human strength can fail and that our trust should rest in Jesus Christ instead.

Like Babylon America wants to build great walls, but these defenses will fail if they are not backed by a wall of prayer. Our prayers to Jesus Christ and obedience to His word are our greatest defense.

I think it is commendable that Donald Trump surrounds himself with pastors and receives prayer. He does not celebrate Ramadan at the Whitehouse but promotes Christmas. This man may have been sent by God, but he could swing either way if the American people and the Church in particular do not repent of their sins and pray for mercy.

There was a leader of the Babylonian empire very similar to President Donald Trump. His name was King Nebuchadnezzar and like Donald Trump he had serious bouts of anger. This man also had a serious issue with pride. He thought of himself as a great builder of an empire. His boasting apparently didn't please God and he was judged.

All this came upon King Nebuchadnezzar. At the end of the twelve months he was

walking about the royal palace of Babylon. The king spoke, saying, "Is not this great Babylon, that I have built for a royal dwelling by my mighty power and for the honor of my majesty?"

Daniel 4:28-30 NKJV

Like King Nebuchadnezzar President Trump has a tendency to throw temper tantrums. This is evident when one looks at the high turn over rate in his cabinet and staff. To be honest I find it almost dizzying the amount of change taking place in Trump's administration. Many are of the opinion President Trump is mentally ill and I would agree. For example, inside Trump's penthouse there are a number of paintings or sculptures to Greek gods/goddesses[ix]. Among them is the ancient Greek god Apollo. I studied up on the god Apollo and found out he was known to have golden hair. I believe Donald Trump's sense of self-importance is so grand that he dyed his hair gold and identifies with this god Apollo.

When a man has megalomaniac traits it is a dangerous sign of a delusional personality. Therefore, we should not be surprised that Kanye West feels a certain kinship with President Trump for this man has his own gospel and delusions about being a god. This kinship was on display when he was invited to the Oval Office to meet with President Trump[x]. Before President Trump and the media Kanye West ranted on and on about his ideas and had no respect for protocol. While he sat in his chair he slouched before the president. At the end of the event he went over uninvited to hug President Trump. Now some may think this is cute, but it is a sign that respect for authority is at a all time low.

Belshazzar the king made a great feast for a thousand of his lords, and drank wine in the presence of the thousand. While he tasted the wine, Belshazzar gave the command to bring the gold and silver vessels which his father Nebuchadnezzar had taken from the

temple which had been in Jerusalem, that the king and his lords, his wives, and his concubines might drink from them. Then they brought the gold vessels that had been taken from the temple of the house of God which had been in Jerusalem; and the king and his lords, his wives, and his concubines drank from them. They drank wine, and praised the gods of gold and silver, bronze and iron, wood and stone.

Daniel 5:1-4 NKJV

There has been a great deal of anger among Americans and people from other nations. Many feel President Trump is disrespectful towards those who are disabled or those that are of different minority groups. Others complain he is a sexist pig for certain remarks he has made about women in the past. Some simply refer to him as being vile. It may be true that President Trump has been vile at some points in his life, but he does have a reverence for most things Christian. He has defended the celebration of Christmas, prayer at school and the pro-life agenda of Christians. He has also installed two very conservative justices at the U.S. Supreme Court. In fact, President Trump hammered Turkey with economic sanctions and demanded they release a U.S. pastor from prison. This pastor has since been freed and I think this is wonderful news! All of this is great, but I am concerned Donald Trump loves himself more than Jesus Christ, Israel or Christians.

Donald Trump seems to think winning is more important than doing what is right. Donald Trump will resort to name calling his opponents or suing them all in an effort to destroy them. It doesn't appear to me or others that he cares about a civil discussion, but in eliminating his opponents. Many Christians are happy that they have a bulldog like Trump to fight for their causes, but he could just as easily turn around and bite them. Donald Trump seems to vacillate on certain issues for awhile and then charge ahead to accomplish something. This man changes his mind a lot. My greatest concern is that he is willing to win at any cost in creating a Mideast Peace by dividing Israel or pushing ahead with a two-state solution.

Like Belshazzar I do not believe President Trump understands the danger of meddling with Israel's borders. Belshazzar's treatment of the temple vessels showed he lacked an understanding of the holiness of these items and the consequences for handling them in a dishonorable way. Belshazzar and his companions were drinking wine from these vessels. Among these guests were concubines. A concubine is just a nice word for a whore. There is a danger in mishandling the things of God or showing irreverence for them. I am concerned that President Trump's irreverence for other people and his mistreatment of them may be a character trait that could lead him to be irreverent or too casual with the issue of Israel's borders.

Israel's borders are a serious issue and any attempt to decrease Israel's size will bring serious consequences!

In the same hour the fingers of a man's hand appeared and wrote opposite the lampstand on the plaster of the wall of the king's palace; and the king saw the part of the hand that wrote. Then the king's countenance changed, and his thoughts troubled him, so that the joints of his hips were loosened and his knees knocked against each other. The king cried aloud to bring in the astrologers, the Chaldeans, and the soothsayers. The king spoke, saying to the wise men of Babylon, "Whoever reads this writing, and tells me its interpretation, shall be clothed with purple and have a chain of gold around his neck; he shall be the third ruler in the kingdom."

Daniel 5:5-7 NKJV

As a consequence of Belshazzar's irreverence for the things of God an ominous sign appears. The fingers of a man's hand appear and begins writing a message on the wall. This king who was once careless and lacking respect for things holy has suddenly been schooled in the fear of the Lord! This terrifying sign causes the king to cry out in terror and to call for the sages to interpret the message. God sends signs to warn us and at times to declare our doom. In the case of Belshazzar there is no opportunity to repent. None of his advisors will be able to interpret the message, but an inquiry will be made for Daniel. Daniel served as an advisor to Nebuchadnezzar but was no longer employed by the state. Daniel is brought to the king to interpret this mysterious message. Daniel corrects the king because this king knew how God humbled King Nebuchadnezzar who reigned before him, but he decided to show irreverence for Israel's God anyway. After Daniel rebukes King Belshazzar, he interprets the message as requested.

Then the fingers of the hand were sent from Him, and this writing was written. "And this is the inscription that was written: MENE, MENE, TEKEL, UPHARSIN. This is the interpretation of each word. MENE: God has numbered your kingdom, and finished it; TEKEL: You have been weighed in the balances, and found wanting; PERES: Your kingdom has been divided, and given to the Medes and Persians.

Daniel 5:24-28 NKJV

Daniel has interpreted the message for Belshazzar and declares to him his kingdom is doomed. It will be divided amongst the Medes and Persians. I believe this is the fate of the United States under President Trump if he pushes forth with a two-state solution on the Mideast Peace Plan. Fortunately, Jesus Christ is not done warning the United States. Jesus Christ has sent two signs against President Trump and the United States to indicate what He will do if they do not change course on dividing Israel. In the next chapter we will see what these signs are and what led to them.

Trump's Betrayal of Israel and the Curse on America

This chapter title may seem like a surprise, but this is exactly what has taken place. President Trump not only betrayed Israel, but his Christian constituency which supported his rise to power. In a gesture of goodwill to Israel and the Evangelical base of America President Trump announced his plans to recognize Jerusalem as the capital of Israel and his plans to move the U.S. Embassy to Jerusalem. While this appeared to be a great deal it was in reality a token gesture. It is true that the U.S. moved their embassy to Jerusalem in 2018, but President Trump was not guaranteeing Jerusalem to Israel. His words make it clear he supports negotiations on the final status of Jerusalem and Israel's borders.[xi] On September 26, 2018 President Trump restated his support for a two-state solution on Israel.[xii] This statement took place during the United

Nations fall meeting where he held a news conference with Prime Minister Benjamin Netanyahu of Israel. While it looks like President Trump is a strong ally of Israel he is not doing anything different from other presidents on Israel. He is still for a two-state solution and sees Jerusalem and Israel's border as flexible. Yes, he moved the embassy. But he is going to divide Israel like every other president has attempted to do. In my opinion President Trump has deceived his Evangelical base and the Israeli people. Land for peace has never worked but President Trump wants to pursue that path.

Nikki Haley's Retirement on October 9, 2018

Many were surprised to see Nikki Haley retire from her position as U.S. Ambassador to the U.N. on October 9, 2018. Theories were thrown about as people guessed the reason for her departure. I have a theory for why she retired. I believe Nikki Haley was in disagreement with Jared Kushner and others who supported a two-state solution on Israel. The two-state solution has been around for some time, but I believe Nikki Haley became aware that President Trump was going to make a real move to divide Israel and she couldn't support it. Before this time, it seemed like a promise that would never take place. As a Christian and avid defender of Israel she couldn't pursue such a position. Most Evangelicals are opposed to splitting Israel and she was well aware of this. In her retirement speech she praised Jared Kushner and Ivanka Trump.[xiii] I believe that was a nod to the real power on Israel negotiations and she gracefully retired. Nikki Haley's retirement set in motion Jesus Christ's punishment on America for advancing the two-state solution. I honestly wonder if she was pushed out by President Trump because the next day two significant signs appeared in the U.S. that indicated judgement.

Judgement on the Economy Sign #1
October, 10, 2018

On this date the Dow Jones Industrial Average closed 831.83 points lower.[xiv] This was a hard hit against the stock market and an indication a correction of the stock market was taking place. I don't believe this would be necessary, but the reckless push for a two-state solution in Israel brought it about. The DJIA can keep surging upwards and America's economy can be great, but only if they chose to support a greater Israel and not recognize the fraudulent claims for land coming from the PLO.

Judgement on the Military Sign #2
October, 10, 2018

It is no coincidence that on the same day the stock market took a big hit that the U.S. military did also. Hurricane Michael became a category 4 hurricane and made landfall on October 10, 2018. When this hurricane made landfall the winds it produced resulted in "catastrophic damage" to the Tyndall Air Force Base on the panhandle of Florida.[xv] After the hurricane passed it was determined that many F-22 Raptors were damaged or destroyed. Some estimates are that 10% of the U.S. military's F-22 Raptors were damaged or destroyed.[xvi] The hit on both the economy and military are a sign to America to move away from a two-state solution and to repent of national sins. America must do this, or it will be destroyed for Jesus Christ is at war with America now.

"At that time Michael shall stand up, the great prince who stands watch over the sons of your people;

Daniel 12:1a

In the above verse we can see that the Archangel Michael watches over the Jewish people. I don't believe it is coincidental that the hurricane was named Michael. In fact, I believe Michael the Archangel was behind the stock market fall and the hurricane.

President Trump and America made the grave mistake of continuing on the path of a two-state solution for Israel. Michael the Archangel will continue to assault the economic and military might of America until it repents. If President Trump and America ignore these warning signs and makes the two-state solution a reality the destruction of America is pretty much guaranteed. The U.S. will find itself divided like Israel by an earthquake, civil war or invasion etc. I sincerely hope this does not take place. I wrote this book in the hope that President Trump or those around him would read this book and change course before its too late!

Israel is Holy

When anyone hears of the word "holy" they generally think of moral purity, but the true meaning of holy is "set apart". This is what Israel is to Jesus Christ. Jesus Christ chose Israel to be a pure nation, but it hasn't always succeeded in that task. Many Christian nations had a history of being pure in God but lost it over time also. Even though Israel has lost its purity it still remains holy or set apart to Jesus Christ and God the Father. Satan knows this and hates Israel and the Jewish people with an unending anger. Satan knows the commandments of God and Jesus Christ came through the Jewish people. Jesus Christ came as the king of the Jews and defeated Satan at the cross. As a defeated foe Satan knows his time is short and is on a campaign to destroy the Jewish people and their promise of a Promised Land.

And war broke out in heaven: Michael and his angels fought with the dragon; and the

dragon and his angels fought, but they did not prevail, nor was a place found for them in heaven any longer. So the great dragon was cast out, that serpent of old, called the Devil and Satan, who deceives the whole world; he was cast to the earth, and his angels were cast out with him. Now when the dragon saw that he had been cast to the earth, he persecuted the woman who gave birth to the male Child. But the woman was given two wings of a great eagle, that she might fly into the wilderness to her place, where she is nourished for a time and times and half a time, from the presence of the serpent.

Revelation 12:7-9, 13-14 NKJV

Unfortunately, most politicians including President Trump don't see the troubles centered around Israel as a spiritual issue. But from the book of Revelation we can clearly see that Israel's protector the Archangel Michael is at war with Israel's persecutor Satan. Israel has been persecuted through the centuries and is constantly persecuted at the U.N. Israel is constantly singled out for criticism at the U.N. when other nations that are far eviler have their crimes ignored. This is hypocritical and shows us that Satan the ruler of this present world is able to instigate nearly all nations against Israel.

As a Canadian I was proud to have Prime Minister Stephen Harper as my national leader. He stood against anti-Semitism and the campaign of misinformation to portray Israel as some apartheid state. This man made Canada a friend of Israel, but now we have gone back to our old ways of siding with the Palestinians under the new Liberal government led by Prime Minister Justin Trudeau. On May 16, 2018 Prime Minister Justin Trudeau chastised Israel for their use of live ammunition in dealing with Palestinian protestors before an actual inquiry had been carried out.[xvii] A lot of these so-called protestors are infiltrating the protest and employing weapons against IDF soldiers. They are simply terrorists and Israeli soldiers must defend themselves. You may recall how God treats people when it comes to Israel. If a nation or person unfairly attacks Israel, they will reap what they have sown. This has happened to my nation of Canada. After Justin Trudeau's unfair assessment of Israel using live ammunition and ignoring the terrorists we have seen gun violence sky rocket in Canada.[xviii] We have also seen acts of terrorism that my government is trying to conceal as incidents of mentally ill people going on a rampage, but this is a lie and cover up.[xix]

How we treat Israel is very important and reveals whether we are aligned with Jesus Christ or Satan. Nations and individuals have risen and fallen based on how they treated Israel. My greatest concern and reason for writing this book is that President Trump thinks he can make a deal in the Mideast where he can create a two-state solution.

This is earthly wisdom and completely unwise when the U.S. is already so divisive. To divide Israel would be like putting the final nail in the coffin and burying America. It would never rise again, and God would destroy America in revenge. Jesus Christ is watching over Israel very closely and watching how we treat Israel.

For thus says the Lord of hosts: "He sent Me after glory, to the nations which plunder you; for he who touches you touches the apple of His eye.

Zechariah 2:8 NKJV

There are many that are arguing that the Palestinians have some right of return, but this is a fraud. Only Israel has the right of return and God promised He would return Israel back to their land when they repented of their sins. In 1948 Israel became a nation again and the U.S. evolved into the world's super power. America's greatness was realized because they made the land of Israel a reality again and provided a place for the Jews to dwell. Giving Israel their land caused America to become very powerful in the world, but in recent years America wants to take back what they have given. Under President Obama and continuing under President Trump the push for a two-state solution has been increasing dramatically, but the disunity within the nation of America has accelerated even as the two-state solution for Israel is being discussed.

"Now it shall come to pass, when all these things come upon you, the blessing and the curse which I have set before you, and you call them to mind among all the nations where the Lord your God drives you, and you return to the Lord your God and obey His voice, according to all I command you today, you and your children, with all your heart and with all your soul, that the Lord your God will bring you back from captivity, and have compassion on you, and gather you again from all the nations where the

Lord your God has scattered you. If any of you are driven out to the farthest parts under heaven, from there the Lord your God will gather you, and from there He will bring you. Then the Lord your God will bring you to the land which your fathers possessed, and you shall possess it. He will prosper you and multiply you more than your fathers. And the Lord your God will circumcise your heart and the heart of your descendants, to love the Lord your God with all your heart and with all your soul, that you may live.

Deuteronomy 30:1-6 NKJV

Here we see in the word of God the ironclad agreement God has made with Israel. God assures them that anytime they repent and turn from their sin He will return them to their fathers' land. In fact, He tells them that it is theirs to possess! Therefore, Israel does not need approval from any nation or international body to dwell in, retain or possess any land historically theirs.

Any nation seeking to interfere with Israel's inheritance will find itself at war with God.

One must understand that Israel is not just another nation. It is a unique nation with a people of great talents. This small people group has acquired quite a number of Nobel prizes for a nation its size.[xx] Throughout its history the Israeli people have risen to the highest places in politics, entertainment, education, law and other pursuits. They are often envied because of the blessing and favor upon them, but any other nationality can become great by blessing Israel. Those nations which strengthen and bless Israel become strong, but those who curse, criticize or weaken Israel usually come to ruin. If America and President Trump are to remain great it must perceive the greatness of Israel. Giving their land away to a barbaric and hateful people inside the West Bank will not bring peace, but only war.

i https://www.toddstarnes.com/show/biden-calls-trump-supporters-virulent-dregs-of-society/

ii
https://www.usatoday.com/story/news/politics/onpolitics/2018/10/09/hillary-clinton-cnn-interview/1578636002/
iii https://www.youtube.com/watch?v=t3CRsnMf1xQ
iv https://www.youtube.com/watch?v=3l2Qfqs10BQ
v https://www.youtube.com/watch?v=mjZFl5-2N_A
vi https://en.wikipedia.org/wiki/Defense_of_Marriage_Act
vii https://www.cnbc.com/2018/09/07/how-trump-has-set-economic-growth-on-fire.html

viii http://www.livius.org/sources/content/herodotus/cyrus-takes-babylon/
ix https://www.dailymail.co.uk/news/article-3303819/Inside-Donald-Trump-s-100m-penthouse-lots-marble-gold-rimmed-cups-son-s-toy-personalized-Mercedes-15-000-book-risqu-statues.html
x https://www.youtube.com/watch?v=jLmQ57mEGFs
xi https://www.whitehouse.gov/briefings-statements/statement-president-trump-jerusalem/
xii https://www.youtube.com/watch?v=61PPhs52S4M
xiii https://www.youtube.com/watch?v=R8PZ8DIAJ5s&t=5s
xiv https://www.cnbc.com/2018/10/10/us-markets-bond-yields-and-data-in-focus.html
xv https://www.apnews.com/c38d3a64213841559102387c42d49cca
xvi https://thediplomat.com/2018/10/nearly-10-percent-of-the-us-f-22-inventory-was-damaged-or-destroyed-in-hurricane-michael/
xvii https://www.cbc.ca/news/politics/trudeau-statement-gaza-independent-investigation-1.4665858
xviii https://www.cnn.com/2018/07/23/americas/toronto-gun-violence-shootings/index.html
xix http://www1.cbn.com/cbnnews/world/2018/july/toronto-killer-mentally-ill-or-isis-terrorist
xx
https://en.wikipedia.org/wiki/List_of_countries_by_Nobel_laureates_per_capita